Disclaimer
The information in this book about healthy lifestyle habits is written for informational and educational use only. It does not constitute medical advice and should not be used as a substitute for medical advice. If your child suffers from any medical condition or if you have any concern at all, always consult with your child's treating doctor and follow your doctor's individualised advice.

Copyright © Keen Kids Education
Text & concept: Dr. Alexandra Bernhardi, 2022
Music: Reuben Dwyer, 2022
Illustrations: Tropic Studio, 2022

Published in 2022 by Keen Kids Education
ISBN   978-0-6455556-0-8

Keen to know more?

Go to www.keenkids.com.au for games, music and more fun stuff.

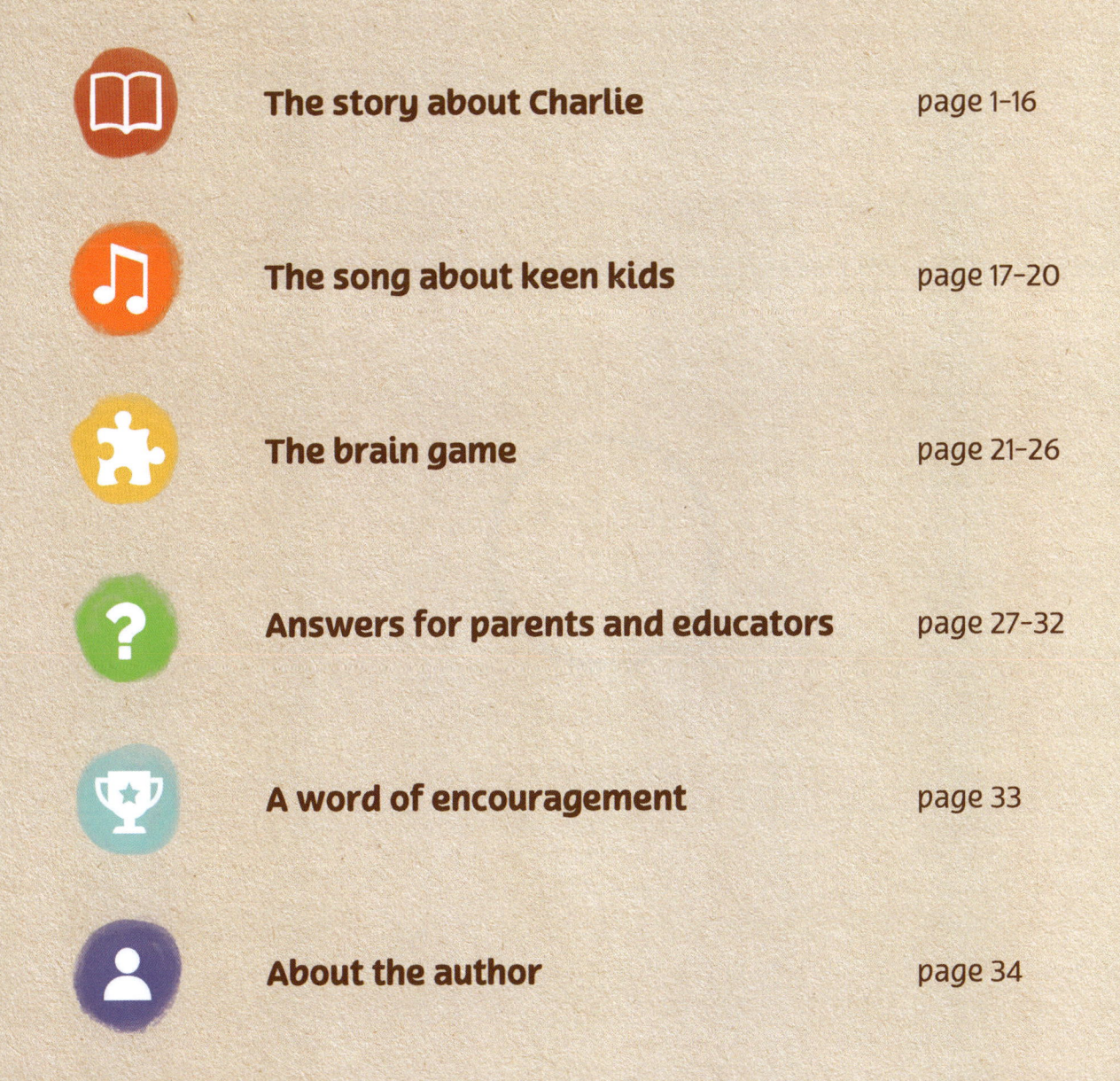

📖	**The story about Charlie**	page 1–16
🎵	**The song about keen kids**	page 17–20
🧩	**The brain game**	page 21–26
❓	**Answers for parents and educators**	page 27–32
🏆	**A word of encouragement**	page 33
👤	**About the author**	page 34

 **The story about Charlie**

This is a story about Charlie, who is a child like you.

What is your name?

_ _ _ _ _ _ _ _ _ _ _ _ _ _ _ _ _ _ _ _

Mr. Y is a very old and wise octopus. He has nine brains and three hearts.

Mr. Y will tell Charlie the secret of how to become a keen kid – happy, strong and smart.

"Do you want to know the secret too?"

Charlie was dreaming about what to become as a grown-up.

A doctor!

A detective!

A firefighter!

♪ But are you smart, brave or strong enough?

Charlie was rather forgetful, afraid of monsters and always out of breath when playing sports.

"Hey Charlie, why don't you become a keen kid? Then you can be anything you want to be. Let me tell you what keen kids do."

Your brain is busy storing away everything you saw, heard and felt during the day – like when you tidy up your room.

Little buddies in your belly clean up the leftovers from all the food you have eaten during the day.

Now you are ready to start a new day.

Every time you use your muscles, they grow.
This makes you stronger.

Trees, flowers and butterflies are your friends.
They help you feel happy.

When you play outside, your immune system learns to fight off bad bugs.
This will help you stay healthy.

Charlie was thinking:
"Hmm, what do keen kids eat?"

Keen kids eat food from the rainbow.

♪ Like lollies and ice cream?

Most healthy foods grow on trees and bushes or you can pick them from the earth.

If you eat healthy food from the rainbow, you'll become strong and smart because all fruits and vegetables have magic powers.

What do plants need to grow?

What do animals drink?

And what should we drink?

When you drink plenty of water, you can think smarter, run faster and poop better.

The bird dropped an empty chips packet on the ground and complained:

♪ Are we done now?

Keen kids are kind to the Earth.

"There is one more thing."

Real food is not only healthier for us but also helps keep our environment clean. Charlie smiled: "Yes, this apple does not need extra wrapping."

A clean Earth keeps our animals happy and healthy too.

It is just so easy.

Let's try it all together:

Keen kids have fun while they play and run.

Keen kids eat food from the rainbow.

Keen kids drink water for thirst.

Keen kids sleep deep like sheep.

Keen kids are kind to the Earth.

♪ Fruit and veggies ♪ Sleep and water ♪ Fun and run

"Now I know what to do to become a keen kid. I can be happy, strong and smart and can become anything I want to be. And you can do it too."

 ## The song about keen kids

Music increases happiness and strengthens learning and memory. You can watch the music video here:
www.keenkids.com.au
Sing, play, hum, clap or dance along – it is fun!

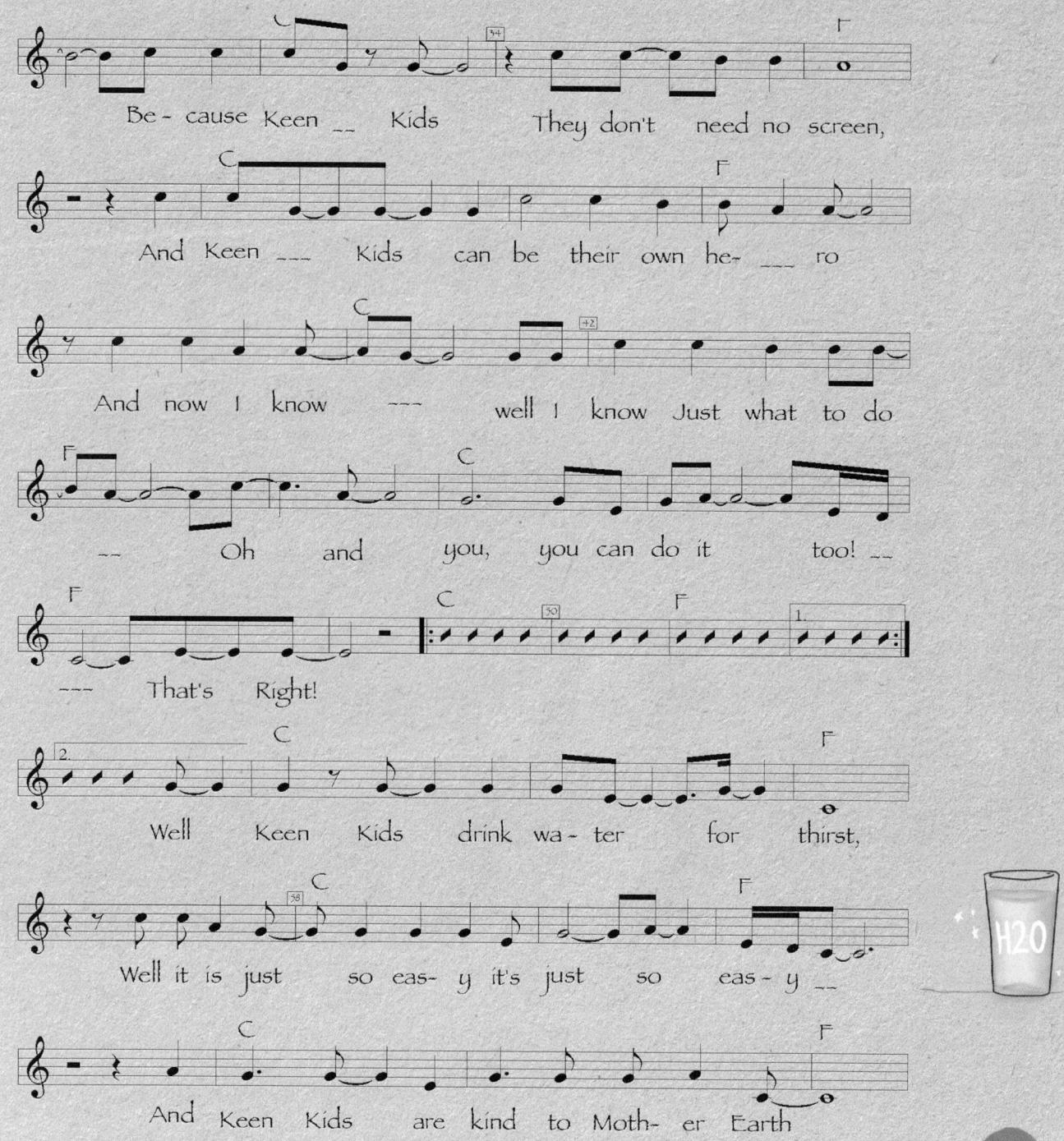

 **The picture brain game**

- Brain games and puzzles have shown to increase attention span and focus.
- Playing these games will help consolidate the messages from the story.
- Children can apply what they have learned from the brain games into day-to-day activities.

How to play:
- Read the headline above the picture.
- Choose one prompt at a time from the list below the picture and give your child time to find it in the scene.
- Feel free to modify the cues to your situation.

You can take this opportunity to discuss the relevance of the actions and also refer back to the story.

What do you do before you go to bed?

- Turn off your tablet
- Tidy up your room
- Read a book
- Close the curtains
- Switch the light off

What else do **you** do before you go to bed?

What fun activities can you do outside?

- Go down the slide
- Kick a ball
- Play jump-rope
- Ride a scooter
- Fly a kite

> What other games do you like to play outside?

Which food is yummy and healthy?

- Cucumbers
- Strawberries
- Bananas
- Apples
- Carrots

Which other rainbow food do you love?

What needs water to grow?

- Children
- Chickens
- Horses
- Trees
- Vegetables

What do **you** need water for?

What does not belong in the ocean?

- Cans
- Plastic bags
- Lolly wrappers
- Plastic bottles
- Chips packets

What do you think should stay out of the ocean?

# Answers for parents and educators

Charlie, the main character in the story 'Charlie the keen kid', manages to develop into an enthusiastic and capable child. Charlie builds resilience and confidence by embracing natural lifestyle habits; habits which have disappeared in our busy society over time.

The brand **keen kids** has been designed to deliver universal and holistic health education. Its goal is to point out and explain simple lifestyle habits which will have a positive effect on children's health and wellbeing, both physically and mentally. Following these achievable and intuitive concepts will help children become what and who they want to be.

While the explanations that Mr. Y gives in the story sound quite simplified, each one of these messages has well-researched science behind it.

In order to be able to answer the many 'why' questions that your child will likely ask, the following information will be helpful for you.

Sleep

Sleep is an important part of our daily biological rhythm and is necessary to maintain and reset our physical and mental functions.

Why do I need to go to bed?

- The brain needs time to sort and process the day's information in order to form long-term memories.
- The release of many hormones is based on your body's internal clock. The majority of Growth Hormone (GH), for example, is released in pulses when you sleep. GH plays a key role in bone and muscle growth, cell repair and metabolism.
- Sleep enhances your immune defence and helps the body fight inflammation, infection and trauma.
- The gut needs a break at night to recuperate from processing food during the day.

What happens if I don't sleep?

- Insufficient or disturbed sleep can lead to many chronic diseases and significantly affects our health and wellbeing far beyond the notion of tiredness.
- People who are sleep-deprived have more problems concentrating due to 'brain fog' and are more vulnerable to depression and anxiety. They also tend to make bad food choices which can lead to obesity, diabetes and heart disease.

How do I set my child up for a good night's sleep?

- The body works best if you go to bed at roughly the same time each night.
- Include foods that help deliver the right nutrients for the body to produce melatonin such as oats, natural cherries, walnuts and chickpea hummus.
- Avoid screen time 2 hours prior - the blue light interferes with the production of melatonin which is our body's natural sleep-inducing hormone.
- Run a warm bath with magnesium or essential oils (e.g. valerian, chamomile or lavender).
- Dim all lights and reduce noise.
- Develop a bedtime routine and end with reading a book with your child.

Active outdoor play

Active outdoor play is important for many aspects of children's development. These include the development of gross and fine motor skills, as well as a healthy immune system.

Why do I need to play outside?
- Being physically active is important for the healthy development of bones, muscles and balance.
- Movement of any kind also improves mental health as it reduces stress. Nature in particular has a calming effect on people.
- Being exposed to soil, which contains many microorganisms, helps children develop a healthy immune system by activating their defence system.
- Exposure to sunlight in a safe way (taking into account individualised skin cancer prevention recommendations) is vital for the body to produce Vitamin D, a key factor for healthy immunity and strong bones.
- Sunlight also regulates the production of melatonin which is an essential sleep-inducing hormone.
- Playfully engaging with other children or being part of a team increases self-worth and helps develop social skills.

What happens if I don't play outside?
- Children who become 'couch potatoes' are at risk of being deficient in Vitamin D which can affect their immune system, bone health as well as mental health.
- They are likely to get sick more often, struggle with their body weight and develop chronic diseases later in life.

How do I get my child to play more outdoors?
- Create an outdoor activity jar based on your circumstances.
- Make outdoor activities part of your routine.
- Join them whenever possible!

A healthy wholefood diet

Eating healthy food is one of the most important factors in raising healthy children. The body relies on the right amount of calories for energy, fibre to feed the good bowel bacteria and micronutrients to sustain cell health.

Why do I need to eat my veggies?
- Vegetables in their whole form contain lots of fibre and micronutrients while being on the lower side of energy density.
- Processed foods on the other hand are low in essential nutrients and contain added chemicals, unhealthy fats, salts and sugars.
- Veggies and fruits come in different colours. Each colour stands for different plant compounds that help to fight cancer, support immunity and reduce inflammation. If you include fruits and veggies with different colours, you will get the whole range of health-supporting nutrients without being a chemistry whiz.
- Vegetables and other plant foods like wholegrains, nuts, seeds, fruits and legumes are rich in fibre. They feed and nourish the good bacteria in your gut. Your gut is involved in keeping the body healthy and in balance, and even has direct communication lines to the brain.

What happens if I don't eat natural food?
Children who do not eat a balanced diet which includes a variety of fruits and vegetables often suffer from an inadequate intake of fibre, vitamins and minerals. This can lead to many problems including:
- Being underweight or overweight
- Behavioural problems
- Problems with emotional and psychological development
- Poor concentration or difficulties at school

How do I get my child to eat more veggies?
- Set up a family routine around healthy wholefoods.
- Get your child involved in selecting and preparing meals when possible.
- Make your own healthy treats based on healthy fruits like frozen fruit paddle pops.
- Be patient and happy with baby steps - this is not a race but a way of living.

Water

The body relies on water to function properly and is an essential part of a healthy, balanced diet. An average child's body is made up of approximately 60% of water.

Why should I drink water?

- The body loses water through breathing, sweating and digestion so we need to replace it daily.
- Water helps regulate body temperature.
- Water helps protect the spinal cord and the brain.
- Water acts as a lubricant and cushion for your joints.
- Water helps the body remove waste.
- Water helps break down the food you eat, allowing the nutrients to be absorbed into your body.
- Water is readily available, inexpensive and free of unwanted sugars and empty calories.

What if I don't drink water?

- If you don't drink water, you become dehydrated and your urine looks darker.
- Dehydration can contribute to headaches, chronic pain, constipation and cognitive problems. Severe dehydration can be fatal.
- Drinking juice and soft drinks will add a significant amount of unwanted sugars, calories and added chemicals into your diet.

How can I get my child to drink more water?

- Filter tap water if required and store it in a glass or stainless steel bottle.
- Add berries or sliced orange to give it some colour and flavour.
- Use a soda maker if your child prefers sparkling water.

Environmental consciousness

A healthy environment is an integral part of human health. Children in particular are highly susceptible to any sort of toxins.

Why are we children so sensitive to pollution?

- Children eat more food, drink more fluids and breathe more air per kilogram of body weight than adults. Children also have a larger skin surface in proportion to their body size than adults. This means that their exposure to harm-causing substances is greater for their size compared to adults.
- Young children naturally explore their environment by putting objects in their mouth and are closer to the ground, thereby frequently exposing themselves to possible toxins.
- Children are also more susceptible to the effects of toxins because their organs, such as their brains and livers, are still growing while at the same time their immune system and detoxification system are still developing and not fully functional.

What happens if the environment is polluted?

- Exposure to air pollution impacts neuro-development and cognitive ability, and can trigger asthma and childhood cancer. Children who have been exposed to high levels of air pollution are at greater risk to develop chronic diseases later in life, such as cardiovascular disease.
- Exposure to a variety of other toxicants such as mercury, lead, organophosphates and persistent organic compounds (POC) can come from ingestion of contaminated food and water, agricultural spray drift, household chemicals, clothing, furniture and personal care products. All these substances can interfere with the development of your child's organs and cause immediate and long-term health concerns.

How can I best protect my child?

- Buy as much locally grown wholefood as possible. This reduces transport- and manufacturing-related pollution.
- Buy food that doesn't require packaging to reduce waste.
- Buy organic food when possible (and reasonable) to minimise exposure to pesticides.
- Use glass or stainless steel containers for food storage.
- Use simple and natural cleaning agents.
- Buy clothing made from natural and untreated material, and don't shy away from secondhand clothes.

A word of encouragement

Congratulations for choosing this book and making healthy lifestyle habits a priority.

You may have identified a couple of areas that you would like to work on or you may have realised that your busy life has taken you down a different pathway and you want to get back on track. We all know how tricky it can be to unlearn old habits and form new and better ones. The following strategies will make it easier for you:

- Be clear about your goals and define the habits that you need to adapt in order to reach them. For example, in order to eat a healthier diet (goal), you will first need to buy fresh vegetables (habit).
- Visualise your goals. Ask yourself, can you see your child as a healthy and successful young adult in their chosen work environment?
- Only change one habit at a time. This way you don't feel overwhelmed. Once this habit has become a routine, move on to the next one.
- Start with the easiest habit. This way you set your child and yourself up for success.
- Start small. If your child struggles to fall asleep before 10pm, move your goal forward in 15 minute increments instead of setting a 7pm bedtime overnight.
- Reward yourself and your child along the way. Create a list with small rewards that align with your new goals and choose one for each step you have mastered.
- Be patient and persistent. Forming new habits requires repetition until it has become a routine that no longer needs any thinking or willpower.
- When you slip, get back on track quickly. Missing your habit once has no measurable impact on your long-term progress.

Forming healthy lifestyle habits is not a race - they are there for good.

All parents want the best for their children. Luckily, when it comes down to leading a healthy and successful life, what's best for the children is also best for us adults. Sometimes, we just need a gentle reminder. All what you need to do now is take the next step. It will be your win.

About the author

Dr. Alexandra Bernhardi is a General Practitioner ('Family Doctor') based in Queensland, Australia. She specialises in Integrative Medicine and enjoys getting to the root cause of diseases while staying on top of emerging science with an open mind.

- Dr. Alex grew up in Germany and studied medicine at Hannover Medical School, complemented by further education in acupuncture and naturopathy.
- She completed a doctoral thesis ('PhD med') in the field of obstetrics in 1999.
- Dr. Alex moved to Australia in 2005 with her three young children and attained Fellowship of the Royal Australian College of General Practice (RACGP) in 2009.
- She joined the Australasian College for Nutritional and Environmental Medicine (ACNEM) in 2015 and regularly undertakes specialised training in all aspects of Integrative Medicine - a modality that combines the best of conventional medicine with evidence-based complementary approaches.
- Dr. Alex dedicates a lot of her time to provide patients with objective education, as she believes that each patient's autonomy is an integral part of the patient's healing journey.
- She is fascinated by the complexity of the human body and the similarities between human and global health.
- Raising her own children as a mother and observing and learning from her patients as a doctor has given her deep insights into some of the root causes of our modern lives' problems.
- Dr. Alex is passionate about nutrition and environmental health and believes that children deserve more education about the foundations of good health in order to support their natural motivation of 'doing the right thing'.

Dr. Alex hopes to see this project reach children and educators all over the world and contribute to making their life easier and the world a better place.

"It is easier to build strong children than to repair broken men."

- Frederick Douglass

 ...and sometimes adults need reminders too.

- Prioritise sleep – most of us need 7 to 8 hours.

- Move your body, enjoy daily time in nature and connect with yourself and others.

- Eat unprocessed foods. Include plenty of vegetables and fruits in different colours.

- Drink mostly water.

- Avoid toxins and unnecessary waste. Our health relies on a healthy environment.

Printed in Great Britain
by Amazon